A BIBLE STUDY OF GOD'S NAMES FOR HIS PEOPLE

COMPILED BY HAYES PRESS

Published by:

HAYES PRESS Publisher, Resources & Media,

The Barn, Flaxlands

Royal Wootton Bassett

Swindon, SN4 8DY

United Kingdom

www.hayespress.org

CHAPTER ONE: NAMING THINGS (GEOFF HYDON)

———

Adam and Eve no doubt had to recognize distinctions be-tween the many trees in Eden's garden; but the Lord Him-self distinguished and named only two trees, and that on the ba-sis of the effect of consuming their fruit. They were 'the tree of life' and 'the tree of the knowledge of good and evil'; how impor-tant to tell the difference, and evidently Eve could. God's terms are meaningful and accurate. If only Eve had been content with all the permitted fruits which were evidence of God's abounding grace meeting her every need! Alas, Adam and Eve were not made to live forever and also to have the knowledge of good and evil.

It is one of humanity's peculiarities, often leading to disastrous consequences that we focus too much on some things to the ne-glect of others. Perhaps this is true when we think of the names which God gives to the spiritual matters upon which He wishes His redeemed to feed, grow and bear fruit. We may feed on one or two truths to the exclusion of others of equal importance; or we may fail to distinguish between them, thinking that they all simply mean the same thing. If so, we may grow to be deformed or distorted believers.

Just as today we may readily remember the variant names given by purveyors of foodstuffs to their different wares, so with simi-lar ease we should be able to list the names God has placed upon

His truths for His redeemed. 'People', 'Nation' and 'Kingdom' might come readily to mind and there are more. They are not given by accident, but by design. Surely we are supposed to distinguish different things about the collective people identified by these names, and not just see them as words meaning the same thing. In spiritual things, such lack of discernment is diagnostic of childhood (1). The way to develop such discernment is by the repeated correct use of the Word of God; it is not done by trial and error, but rather by the continuous practice of what is right. See for example the work of the priest in distinguishing between the clean and the unclean (2). We need to work out carefully, therefore, what God is saying in His Word by rightly dividing the Word of Truth and then put our understanding into obedient practice. It is perhaps humbling to think that disciples together should be identifiable by their practices and then recognised as such by the appropriate names, or divine titles, God gives to His followers.

The Consistency in God's Use of Names

In the book of Genesis we find the account of Jacob. Because of Laban's unfair demands Jacob needed a way to distinguish and identify his sheep from those of Laban (3). In due time Jacob's sheep had a different appearance; the difference proving ownership. Of course his and Laban's sheep were all still sheep.

The terms 'sheep' and 'flock' are not limited in the Bible to their natural setting. God loves to use them to indicate different aspects of His spiritual sheep and their relationship to Himself; each is lasting. The description begins in the Old Testament and continues into the New. This series will try to examine such continuity and distinctions in divinely given names. We cannot hope to understand the Word of God correctly if we focus only on the New Testament. There are things that become plainer the more we see the Old Testament previews of the greater New Testament truth, and that is what God intended (4).

The Topics of the Book

The terms we plan to review include: the Chosen Race; the People of God; the Sheep of the Flock; the Vine & Vineyard; the Church; the House of God, the Holy and Royal Priesthood; the Holy Nation; the Kingdom of God.

The series seeks to alert readers to the different meanings which may be hidden in terms that, at first glance, seem similar and to make such discernment a habit in Bible study. By doing so we shall see how it is unique to find one's place among the people described by God in these ways. Thus it is not a matter of intellectual curiosity, but seeking from God the right way to live our lives so that our practices conform to His descriptions of us.

The Need for Care!

Sometimes the same word means different things. For instance, where baptism is mentioned care is needed to determine which type of baptism is meant. When Paul found disciples who had only been baptized (dipped) in water in obedience to John's teaching he instructed them to be baptized again (5). The same word therefore describes two different things, and baptism as a follower of John's teaching could not then substitute for the baptism of a believer as a disciple of Christ. Then Paul describes yet another baptism (6), which Christ now does with each person at the time of their salvation; He baptizes them, not in water but in the Holy Spirit (7), into the church which is His Body. Again, Christ's death, burial and resurrection are called by Him a 'baptism' (8). We obviously need to distinguish between the different situations when this word is used if we are to understand and then act properly as individual disciples. The Bible provides instruction too for disciples seen together as a church.

The churches of God exist today (see www.churchesofgod.info) because in the 19th century some believers saw the need to distinguish carefully between the various uses of the word 'church' in the Scriptures. Many believers saw no difference between the scriptural terms: 'the church which is the Body of Christ' and 'church of God' (9). God provided understanding to those who sought it, so that they were able to see important differences, important because they revealed that some people were in one church but not the other. The different terms were found to contain separate treasures, and failure to distinguish between them had resulted in disadvantages to disciples and less glory to God.

The purpose of this revelation was not to create a small subgroup of believers who had a stronger intellectual grasp of the meaning of Scripture. Rather, it opened again a door for all believers to adopt changed practices that were closer to what the Scriptures say and therefore more God-glorifying. It also showed how errors that brought sorrow to the heart of God could properly be corrected. The introductory point before us here is the need to examine all Scriptural terms with the same care.

Peter wrote to people in churches across a wide area. It is evident when we reach 1 Peter 2:9 that he is describing not just individual Christians, but disciples brought together in united testimony, because he uses collective nouns in each case to describe a unique grouping of people. However, his terms can all too easily be disregarded as synonyms - in much the same way as people had traditionally failed to distinguish between the Church the Body of Christ and the churches of God. We must look for the precise sense God intends us to see in each term, and the particular things we should do to put such truth into practice. Such accuracy is not a mere argument about words; Scripture expects us to see and act upon these special characteristics.

The Challenge

So, as we consider in this book the various names which God has specifically chosen to apply to those He has redeemed, we shall be challenged in each chapter to ask:

"What would God have to do so that the name He has given may accurately apply to His redeemed?" and "What behaviour is expected of those so described, to retain the use of the unique name God gives them?"

Bible References: (1) Hebrews 5:11-14 (2) Leviticus 10:10: Ezekiel 44:23; cf. Ezekiel 22:26; Haggai 2:11-14 (3) Genesis 30,31 (4) Acts 17:11; 2 Peter 1:20,21 (5) Acts 19:3-5 (6) 1 Corinthians 12:13 (7) Matthew 3:11 (8) Luke 12:50 (9) e.g. Ephesians 1:22,23; 1 Corinthians 1:2

CHAPTER TWO: A CHOSEN RACE (EDWIN NEELY)

G od is a God of sovereign choices (1), many of which select the few from very many. From the vastness of space and an innumerable array of galaxies in the universe, all of His creation, God chose the one in which we live. It is so large in its rotation around its centre that it is estimated that it would take the sun 225 million years to make a complete circuit. Our galaxy is 100,000 light years in diameter; and from its profusion of heavenly bodies God chose this planet, so tiny in the diversity and scheme of space.

'Tis on earth the Lord discloses

All His love how vast it is;

Earth's the favoured spot He chooses

To display the truth of this

That God is love. (T. Kelly)

He then chose humanity out of the myriad of living species of this creation (2), and from those that issued from the first Adam He chose the godly line of Seth, through the godly line of Shem, then the godly line of Abraham (3), from whom were born various races. One in particular was God's choice: Israel. Of the vast number of races upon the earth, whom Isaiah describes as 'a drop in a bucket', a speck of 'dust on the scales' (4), God loved Israel because He loved them (5), made a choice, and called them, "Israel whom I have chosen" (6) - not because they were anything, but when they were nothing. When Israel's own choices did not include steadfastness to the ways of God (7), He made a further choice, saying through Peter to New Testament saints who were living stones built up a spiritual house, 'but you are a chosen race' (8).

So important to God and central to His purposes was the choice of His earthly race that the whole of the boundaries of all nations were distributed according to its size and number (9). Empires have risen and fallen in relation to their treatment of Israel, and future world allotment will fall in line with the place that God has given to that earthly chosen race (10). What spiritual riches will be apportioned to the spiritual race so chosen (11) could only beggar the imagination now and will have to wait for eternity to reveal. Israel will become to the world what the shekel of the sanctuary was to be to Israel. All things will be commensurate with it. Such is the importance of the choice of God.

Did all the sons of Seth or Shem or Abraham become an integral part of the elect? Not at all! The choice narrowed to the twelve sons of Jacob and their progeny. Not all of Jacob's children were included in this choice (12). Though the word 'race' may emphasize those with a common father, not all who were fathered by any of the patriarchs were included in God's narrow choice. Not even all those who own God as their heavenly Father find themselves included here (13). Many are called; few are chosen (14). The smallness of God's chosen race has always been a stumbling block, even to earnest seekers after God. What a blessing of grace and mercy to ever be considered a part of that which finds its expression in a people who once were none, but are now the people of God! (15)

God impressed upon Israel that their race was chosen in His sovereignty and not because they were anything (16). Through Paul, God also emphasizes that His present choice involves 'not many wise ... mighty ... noble' (17). One purpose in His choosing the weak and beggarly is to prove to all His infinite wisdom and bring to nothing any wisdom so-called that might be arraigned in opposition (18).

From God's choice race, Israel, He was pleased to bring about the natural birth of Christ (19). Unreceived by His own, but received by those called of the Spirit, He is now head of the Church which is His Body; but more than that, Lord of all who will by obedience align themselves with His truth and His people. Chosen in Christ, we are supplied with boundless blessing here and will be hereafter, and here and now are given the inestimable privilege of divine acceptance and service (20) as the 'elect according to the foreknowledge of God the Father, in sanctification of the Spirit, for obedience and sprinkling of the blood of Jesus Christ' (21). As those who firstly know the working of faith, we then become obedient to the Faith (22) and find ourselves linked with that chosen race. Those of Israel who sidestepped their promise to do all that the LORD had said and be obedient would find themselves cut off from the very race to which they by birth had a right. That rule doesn't change.

The purpose for us of God's choice is variously explained. We have looked at Paul's word to the Corinthians about putting to shame those who are wise with this world's wisdom. But Peter expands this by reminding us that we are to 'proclaim the excellencies of Him who has called [us]out of darkness into His marvelous light' (23). This we do in a two-pronged thrust, extolling God with our united praises, and proclaiming Christ as the only way of salvation to a sin-weary world.

"Behold, My Servant, whom I uphold; My chosen one in whom My soul delights." (24) Some Bible students say that the 'chosen one' here is Israel, as it seems surely to be in verse 19 of the chapter, but Matthew (12:18-21) makes clear that Messiah is the Servant. Israel was necessary, however, to bring about His natural birth. He was the promised 'Star out of Jacob' and will be eventually seen fully as the 'Sceptre out of Israel' (25). But He was to be 'the last Adam' (26), the progenitor of a new race.

It is God's will that all men should 'be saved and to come to the knowledge of the truth' (27). He makes clear, nonetheless, that all men will not be saved (28); neither, very apparently, will all who are saved come to the knowledge of the truth. Those who are without, God judges (29), and our part is neither to judge nor criticize those who are not among us, but one thing God makes very clear is that those who are obedient to the truth are to be numbered among that chosen race. We are chosen 'in [Christ] before the foundation of the world' as far as our salvation is concerned (30). Those who are numbered with this race are also chosen 'according to the foreknowledge of God the Father, by the sanctifying work of the Spirit' (31). Our election to obedience to the Faith requires that we make our election more sure (32), a thing that could in no way happen as far as God's election to eternal salvation is concerned.

Through Christ, God's chosen, we who are chosen in Christ know and shall know the abundance of God's grace in all the brilliant aspects of salvation. Through Christ, God's chosen, we who are chosen for a place among God's chosen race, know the blessings of being built up a spiritual house for a holy priesthood and all the blessings of entrance within the veil and drawing near to God in worship (33), Christ is the corner stone to which individuals, being aligned, will also find their place in the alignment of the building, 'a dwelling of God in the Spirit', that which 'is growing into a holy temple in the Lord' (34).

This realization of God's grace towards us should bring elation, but it must also bring intense humility and a spirit of thankfulness. We are encouraged - indeed, commanded - to ensure a commensurate behaviour towards our fellow saints, each the brother and the sister for whom Christ died, each the brother and the sister that God has chosen to be part of this chosen, holy race.

What, then, have we gleaned? From numbers that surpass human imagination a sovereign God has made choices according to His own wisdom and grace, and each choice has resulted in a decreasing number of chosen ones, until He has at last a chosen race. Those comprising it are all of one Father, are related to each other because of the work of Calvary and an obedience to the faith once for all delivered to the saints. They own Christ as Lord and are built into God's house. In fulfilling their purpose they act concerning God and man, and seek to add to their numbers according to the direction of the Word of God and His Holy Spirit.

The choice of God can be honoured or set aside by those so gathered together, and the appreciation of God's choosing should be a matter of constant praise and consistent humility. The setting aside of the conditions imposed by God can result in expulsion from the race for a time, that there might be repentance, or permanently, should God grant none (35). No greater earthly blessing can be afforded than to be faithful in service among the people of God's chosen race, and heavenly blessings too rich to imagine will forever bless those whose choice is surrendered to God's.

Bible references: (1) E.g. 1 Chronicles 16:13; Ephesians 1:4; Psalm 33:12 (2) Hebrews 2:6 (3) Hebrews 11:8,9,12 (4) Isaiah 40:15-17 (5) Deuteronomy 7:6-8 (6) Isaiah 44:1,2 (7) Deuteronomy 28:45-47 (8) 1 Peter 2:9 (9) Deuteronomy 32:8 (10) Zechariah 14:17 (11) Ephesians 2:7 (12) Genesis 34:1 (13)1 John 2:19 (14) Matthew 22:14 (15) 1 Peter 2:10 (16) Deuteronomy 7:7 (17) 1 Corinthians 1:26 (18) 1 Corinthians 1:20 (19) Matthew 1 (20) 1 Peter 2:5 (21)1 Peter 1:2 (22) Acts 6:7 (23) 1 Peter 2:9 (24) Isaiah 42:1 (25) Numbers 24:17 (26) 1 Corinthians 15:45 (27) 1 Timothy 2:4 (28) Revelation 20:15 (29) 1 Corinthians 5:13 (30) Ephesians 1:4 (31) 1 Peter 1:2 (32) 2 Peter 1:10 (33) Hebrews 10:19 (34) Ephesians 2:21,22 (35) 2 Timothy 2:25

CHAPTER THREE: GOD'S PEOPLE (KEITH DORRICOTT)

Who Are God's People?

When Peter wrote the words, 'you are ... a people for God's own possession' in 1 Peter 2:9, who was he referring to and what did he mean? Isn't this true of everyone? Don't all of us on earth belong to God? He is our Maker (Job 35:10), 'the God of all flesh' (Jer.32:27), and 'we are His offspring' (Acts 17:29). Can anyone be excluded from this term 'God's people'?

Today there are many peoples in the world, with varying characteristics, differentiated by language, culture and background. But it wasn't always that way. Mankind was originally unified, with one language and purpose, but that all changed about four thousand years ago. When men began to build the tower at Babel (in present-day Iraq), God said about it: "'Behold, they are one people, and they all have the same language. And this is what they began to do, and now nothing which they purpose to do will be impossible for them'" (Genesis 11:6). They were united, but apart from God. And so He scattered them and they fragmented into many peoples. Their unity was broken and it has stayed that way ever since, with ever-increasing diversity.

This attitude of independence disqualified mankind in general from being God's special possession. Yet He did not abandon His purpose. He had already chosen the descendants of Abram, from whom came the Israelite people. They became one of many peoples on this earth, but with a distinct identity and purpose. They were 'God's people'; those whom God would be with, and who would be the focus of His attention. What distinguished them was their faith and obedience to God, in contrast with the independence around them. Of them it says, 'God is not ashamed to be called their God' (Hebrews 11:16).

What Does It Mean To Be 'God's People'?

For them and for us today to be God's people means that 'the' one true living God becomes 'our' God. This is distinctly the title that He uses to describe this relationship, rather than 'Lord' or 'Father', etc. ("'I will be their God, and they shall be My people'" - 2 Corinthians 6:16; Hebrews 8:10).

To have God as 'our' God means that He has a special care for us; He calls us 'the apple of His eye' (Zechariah 2:8). He told Israel that He had 'set His love' on them; they were the ones He looked to for His delight ('The LORD takes pleasure in His people' – Psalm 149:4). He wants more than ownership of us - He wants possession, to be the centre of our lives ('You, O LORD, are in the midst of this people, for You, O LORD, are seen eye to eye' – Numbers 14:14), and to be revered and served as the Almighty. He wants us to respond to Him and to follow His direction ("'Oh that My people would listen to Me, that Israel would walk in My ways!'" – Psalm 81:13). He wants to be our God in reality, not just in name. ("I will also walk among you and be your God, and you shall be My people" – Leviticus 26:12). We are His inheritance, the portion of mankind that He can call His own (Deuteronomy 32:9).

In turn God offers us as 'His' people the benefits of His protection (Psalm 125:2), strength and provision for our needs (Deuteronomy 8:7-9). ('The LORD will give strength to His people; the LORD will bless His people with peace' – Psalm 29:11). And so unlike peoples of the world we do not act independently of Him, and He will never desert us ('The LORD will not abandon His people, nor will He forsake His inheritance' – Psalm 94:14). He faithfully keeps all His promises to us. He wants us to be at rest with Him, which is what He has worked for since the time of creation (Hebrews 4:9-11).

What Was Required for Israel to Become God's People?

In God's mind, the Israelites were His people long before He made them a nation under His law at Sinai. He had known them beforehand and He promised them to Abraham, Isaac and Jacob (Israel). Years later He explained: '"The LORD did not set His love on you nor choose you because you were more in number than any of the peoples, for you were the fewest of all peoples, but because the LORD loved you and kept the oath which He swore to your forefathers, the LORD brought you out by a mighty hand and redeemed you from the house of slavery"' (Deuteronomy 7:7,8).

Even when Pharaoh was their master in Egypt, they were still referred to as God's people. Hebrews 11:25 tells us that Moses chose 'rather to endure ill-treatment with the people of God, than to enjoy the passing pleasures of sin'. And when God confronted Pharaoh through Moses, the demand was, "Let My people go ..." (Exodus 5:1).

And so even in Egypt they were distinct. When He was about to bring them out God said to them, "I will take you for My people, and I will be your God; and you shall know that I am the LORD your God, who brought you out from under the burdens of the Egyptians" (Exodus 6:7). At the Passover, when the Israelite firstborn were preserved by the covering blood, no such provision was made for the Egyptians – "... that you may understand how the LORD makes a distinction between Egypt and Israel" (Exodus 11:7).

In the wilderness, after they had received and accepted the covenant which united them as a people serving God, Israel was described as "a people who dwells apart, and shall not be reckoned among the nations" (Numbers 23:9). Prior to their entering the land, after hearing all the Lord's commands, that generation was told, "This day you have become a people for the LORD your God" (Deuteronomy 27:9). He had separated them to Himself, and they had pledged obedience to Him. They were ready to fulfill His desire for them. But, had it ended there, we today who are Gentiles could have had no part in it.

Can We Today Become God's People?

Israel had been told that it was sadly possible for any one of them to be cut off from the people of God, for such things as immorality, blasphemy, uncleanness and failure to take the distinguishing mark of circumcision. Godly lives were demanded of a people belonging to God ("... 'Be holy; for I am holy ...'" Leviticus 11:44). Eventually the ungodliness and unbelief of Israel culminated in their rejection of their Messiah when He came, resulting in the great majority of them being cut off. But then in His mercy God allowed believing Gentiles, who previously had no claim to Him being their God, to be included, for He is the God of Gentiles as well as of Jews (Romans 3:29). Which is why Peter wrote in 1 Peter 2:10: 'You once were not a people, but now you are the people of God; you had not received mercy, but now you have received mercy'.

But we are warned in Romans 11:22 that, just as Israel lost the privilege, so can we: 'Behold then the kindness and severity of God; to those who fell, severity, but to you, God's kindness, if you continue in His kindness; otherwise you also will be cut off.' Faithfulness and godliness are just as vital to our continuing to be His special possession today.

What Was Required To Make Us God's People?

Just as Israel had to be redeemed from Egypt to function as God's people, so we have had to be redeemed and purified - by the sacrifice of Christ: 'Our great God and Savior, Christ Jesus ... gave Himself for us that He might redeem us from every lawless deed, and to purify for Himself a people for His own possession, zealous for good deeds' (Titus 2:13,14).

His sacrifice has also sanctified us to be God's people - set us apart, separated us to God, from this world of godlessness, distinct from all other peoples. It is by the death and resurrection of Jesus Christ that 'His' God has become 'our' God (John 20:17). He has purchased us and called us to Himself, to be gathered together as 'the church of the living God' - the called-out assembly of the people of God on earth today (1 Timothy 3:15). So that God's people today, as in the past, can be united in service to Him.

And so, as Hebrews 13:11-13 explains, the place of God's people today is outside the things of the world. 'For the bodies of those animals whose blood is brought into the holy place by the high priest as an offering for sin, are burned outside the camp. Therefore Jesus also, that He might sanctify the people through His own blood, suffered outside the gate ... So, let us go out to Him outside the camp, bearing His reproach. This world is a defiled place and God's people must be kept from everything ungodly while living in it. God says "I will dwell in them and walk among them; and I will be their God, and they shall be My people. Therefore, come out from their midst and be separate," says the Lord. "And do not touch what is unclean; and I will welcome you"' (2 Corinthians 6:16,17).

And so years ago God set aside the rest of mankind in their unbelief but accepted Israel. Then He set aside most of Israel in their unfaithfulness but accepted us. As we remain faithful we today are also allowed to have this term apply to us, to be God's special possession, to receive His special care and enjoy His presence, distinct among the peoples of this world. Because we are 'God's people', in the fullest sense, and He is truly 'our God'.

CHAPTER FOUR: SHEEP AND THE SHEPHERD (ROBERT SHAW)

———

Isn't it interesting that a great deal of the simile and metaphor of Scripture relates to country life? Examples include the sowing of seed, the harvesting of crops, of fruit, of vineyards and narrative surrounding both domestic and wild animals. Of course, many to whom the messages of Scripture first came were country folk, familiar with these things. Often, basic laws and practices seen in the natural world assist in our understanding of the spiritual. The subject before us is one of these.

Sheep And The Shepherd

If what we have said is true regarding similarities with country life, how profound is God's description of human beings as sheep and of Christ as Shepherd. The propensity of humans to go astray like sheep is reflected in well-known passages of Scripture such as Isaiah 53:6, 'All we like sheep have gone astray'; and in Psalm 119:176, 'I have gone astray like a lost sheep'. Sheep may be fearful and timid animals, but we are told they possess a stubborn nature that often leads them into foolish ways and perverse habits.

As with the natural, so in a spiritual sense: by their sinful nature, human beings are like lost sheep. As He went about all the cities and villages surrounding the sea of Galilee, Jesus was moved with compassion for the multitudes 'because they were weary and scattered, like sheep having no shepherd' (Matthew 9:36). It was for such that He had come to die. He said, "I am the good shepherd. The good shepherd gives His life for the sheep" (John 10:11). Trusting in Christ we are His - His by virtue of purchase. He gave His life for us. We are sharers in the life of Christ; we are intimately identified with Him. He is the Good Shepherd in death, the Great Shepherd in resurrection (Hebrews 13:20) and the Chief Shepherd at His coming again (1 Peter 5:4).

What a comfort it is to be able to say with certainty, 'the LORD is my shepherd', describing that personal relationship that exists between the believer and the Lord. The rich provision described so bountifully in Psalm 23 has been a source of comfort and joy to many in successive generations.

Sheep Together As A Flock

Of course it is almost unnatural that a sheep should exist alone. It was not made that way. The analogy of sheep presupposes a number of them together with a relationship to one another. So we recognise in Scripture our Lord's purpose to bring His sheep together as one flock. It is ever His intention that those whom He calls "'My sheep'", believers in our Lord Jesus, should be called by name and led by Him. His words in John 10:16 confirm that purpose. He said, "there will be one flock and one shepherd". Sadly, many do not follow.

What brings sheep together as one flock is their response to the voice of the shepherd. There may be many folds into which sheep have been brought - and many flocks - but sheep that know their shepherd will gather together from such folds and flocks into one flock when they hear his voice. It is a distinctive voice. Again, Jesus declared in John 10:16, "they will hear My voice". In divine purpose there is only one Shepherd and one flock. This divine principle found expression also in Old Testament days. Psalm 100:3 says, 'We are His people and the sheep of His pasture' and Psalm 79:13 says, 'Your people and sheep of Your pasture, will give You thanks forever; we will show forth Your praise to all generations'. Such scriptures demonstrate the distinctive nature of those gathered to His pasture.

God has a design and purpose for His gathered flock today over which He exercises the authority of pastoral care. The Lord calls them the 'little flock' (Luke 12:32), possibly because there were few who were willing to hear His voice and obey the call of the Shepherd. Peter calls them 'the flock of God' and, because of the One to whom they belonged, he knew how important it was in shepherd care to be seen as examples to the flock (1 Peter 5:2,3).

Caring for the Flock

We understand that, more than any other livestock, sheep need constant attention and care. They are subject to fear, tension and aggravation from external influences. On the other hand they prosper in calm surroundings.

The Chief Shepherd, loving His flock as He does, appoints under-shepherds to exercise care on His behalf. 1 Peter 5:1-4 teaches that it is the work of overseers to care for His flock. By His Spirit, God put earnest care into the heart of a young man called Titus, enabling him not only to minister to the Church in

Corinth (2 Corinthians 8:16) but to carry out a difficult assignment for the Lord (Titus 1:5). Thus He equips His willing shepherds.

We have already noted that Christ is also the Good Shepherd. The word 'good' in Greek is 'kalos', meaning 'beautiful' or something 'intrinsically excellent'. The same word is used for the work of oversight in 1 Timothy 3:1. It is a 'beautiful' work. What a privilege that those called to do the service of under-shepherds can reflect the beautiful character of Christ.

Peter, who had earlier denied his Master in the courtyard of the high priest, had received a vital lesson from the Lord. John 21:15-17 reveals the question the Lord asked him three times, "Simon, ... do you love Me?" Following Peter's strong affirmation, the Lord commanded, "Feed My lambs"; "Tend My sheep"; "Feed My sheep". The sheep were His. Peter could never truly have tended and fed them, demonstrating love for them, had he not unequivocally loved their Owner. The shepherds must first of all care for the sheep out of love for the Chief Shepherd.

Enthusiastically, David revealed to king Saul his credentials as a fearless soldier of the living God. In 1 Samuel 17:34,35 he explained his conquests of the enemies of his father's flock. "Your servant used to keep his father's sheep, and when a lion or a bear came and took a lamb out of the flock, I went out after it and struck it, and delivered the lamb from its mouth". There is here no expression of wound or injury to the shepherd. His whole focus is highlighting the safety of the sheep, exercising God-given strength, born out of deep affection for the flock and its Owner.

Feeding the Flock

This is an essential aspect of care. Many scriptures refer to pasture land as feeding for the sheep. Delivering it is a great responsibility for the shepherd, leading the flock under his care to rich pastures where health and stamina can be maintained by the quantity and quality of the food. It has been said that pasture in Israel was not naturally in abundance. It was often provided by the laborious work of the shepherd who cultivated rich pasture from what had formerly been dry and arid land. Shepherds themselves need to be painstakingly committed men.

When Ezra, with the priests and Levites, read from the law of the LORD in the open square from morning until midday (Nehemiah 8:3) it was not a mere recital. They had obviously spent time with the Word and so could help the people to understand the reading. How much material has the Spirit of God to work with from the store of the Word in shepherd hearts? Has it grown over the years? Are shepherds able to gather from their store to feed the sheep with the right food for their growth and development?

David was taken from the sheepfolds to shepherd Israel. Psalm 78 tells us that 'he fed them according to the integrity of his heart; and guided them by the skilfulness of his hands' (RV). Here is an example of wholeheartedness. Shepherds of the flock of God today have a God-given responsibility to provide pasture on which lambs and sheep can safely feed and in such a way that their appetite for it will increase rather than diminish. Committed shepherds will take full account of the needs of the sheep to deliver a healthy diet, to give time in its preparation and to be sensitive to the best feeding methods.

Froth generally gathers on the surface and is insubstantial compared with the value of gems that have to be painstakingly dug out. May shepherds hear the clear instruction of Acts 20:28, 'Take heed unto yourselves, and to all the flock ... to feed the church of God' (RV).

The Footsteps of the Flock

There is a lovely passage of Scripture in Song of Songs 1:8. It says, 'Follow in the footsteps of the flock'. What are these footsteps? Before the Lord Jesus returned to heaven He met with His disciples and taught them 'the things pertaining to the kingdom of God' (Acts 1:3). In turn, it was these things that the disciples themselves taught and were engaged in thereafter. Many of them appear in the book called 'The Acts of the Apostles'. Those who received Christ as Lord and Master were baptised and added to the disciples already comprising the little flock. 'They continued steadfastly in the apostles' doctrine and fellowship, in the breaking of bread and in prayers' (Acts 2:42). The apostles' teaching, of course, involves many aspects of divine doctrine contained in their epistles. As we dig into the Word of God by the help of the Holy Spirit we shall find gems of truth to guide us.

Enemies of the Flock

The Lord Jesus spoke to His disciples about the thief and the wolf. He said the thief comes 'to steal, and to kill, and to destroy ... and the wolf catches the sheep and scatters them' (John 10:10-12). Here is reference to the work of the Adversary. Paul had sufficient foresight to see troubles ahead for the little flock, both from the inside and outside. He gave stern warning because of the gravity of overseers arising who would mislead the flock, drawing disciples to themselves. He also warned of wolf-like intruders bent on destruction. What was to be the only defence? As then, so also today it is watchfulness, remembrance of the teaching of the Lord and prayer (Acts 20:31,36).

CHAPTER FIVE: THE REST OF GOD (JOHN TERRELL)

―――

S eeking, as this book does, to explore the special significance of various descriptive terms used in Scripture of the people of God today, we are helped to focus on the remarkable variety and richness of these. This in turn leads us to appreciate more deeply the value the Lord places on a gathered-out community in worship and service for His glory.

The subject of 'The Rest of God' in Scripture, while not strictly presenting a collective term descriptive of God's people, is nonetheless specially applied to such a people in both Old and New Testaments, and sheds its own precious light on the delight and purpose which God has in His people. This is underlined by the fact that most of the New Testament discussion of this subject is given to us in the Epistle to the Hebrews, which is itself the guide to the unique character of God's people today, especially in their priestly service. It paints a picture of a godly condition in which such a people fulfils its unique place in God's gracious purposes today: and it does this by comparing and contrasting Old and New Testament purposes of God, demonstrating the vast superiority of the New Covenant context.

So, what is the Rest of God in the Scriptures, and how can a sanctified and serving people come to enjoy this and be motivated by it to richer service? It is important at this point to underline again the unique association of this matter of God's REST with the people of God. Hebrews 4:9 is a crucial verse here. 'There remains therefore a rest for the people of God'. It is at this point that the author of the Hebrews epistle moves on from the experience of Israel, God's Old Testament people, in respect of the Rest of God, to the Holy Spirit's application of this truth to God's New Covenant people - to those today who share in the privileges and position of house of God and kingdom of God among other important subjects dealt with in this book. The early verses of chapter 4 of Hebrews, following on from a lament on the failure of Old Testament Israel to enter into God's Rest, says, 'Therefore, since a promise remains of entering His rest, let us fear lest any of you seem to have come short of it'.

Now to help us understand the basic concept of the Rest of God it is important to note the meaning and significance of the Greek word mainly used in the Hebrews chapters 3 and 4 references. This is given by linguists as 'resting down' and hence the thought of 'abiding'; which in turn conveys a state of settled abiding. This is important, as we shall see, in today's multiple and widely varying 'homes' for a Christian's service; involving so many disciples of the Lord Jesus in moving from group to group and from 'church' to 'church'. God's purpose is for a place of settled abiding in Christian life and service.

The earliest model and example for us in this is found in the creation story of Genesis. Again our source of reference is in Hebrews - in chapter 4 verse 4 – 'And God rested on the seventh day from all His works'. God's own rest on the seventh day, the Sabbath, was to be an example and pattern for the people of Israel, especially in relation to the land of promise. That land was to be their settled abode to which God had led them through many trials and blessings, and only by settling all their hopes there, with its dwelling place for God at its heart, would they find permanent rest and fulfilment after their wilderness pilgrimage.

We have, of course, to recognise the limitations of this as a type of spiritual experience in New Covenant times, for the Christian today is invited to enter into God's rest for them immediately on receiving the blessing of redemption through faith in Christ and commitment through baptism, to serving God in His house and holy nation, subjects dealt with separately in this book. The vital matter dealt with in Hebrews 3 and 4 is that of entering into God's rest, and the spiritual dangers attendant on failing to do so. 'Entering in' in this context means recognising, and progressively enjoying, the spiritually settled life-style of the people God has ordained for Christian service in our day; not simply making a starting commitment to that place, essential though that is. Readers would be well advised to ponder the words of Hebrews chapters 3 and 4 in particular; for it is here that this important, though often neglected, aspect of the service of God's people in His house is expounded. Central to the whole matter is the warning, repeated several times in these verses, of failing to 'enter into' God's rest of settled and undistracted service; a failure which can overtake the disciple even after he or she has made a commitment to the place itself, and can greatly diminish his enjoyment of it.

God's Old Testament people Israel had a fluctuating experience in the matter at different stages of their history in the land. Hebrews 4:7,8 shows this to have been so after the tragedy had occurred in which a whole generation who came out of Egypt had not even entered physically into the promised land, much less entering in a settled way into the spiritual privileges God had for them. This is typified by their failure to take possession, literally, of large tracts of the territory promised to them. It is primarily concerning their spiritual experience that teaching and warning comes down to us today.

In the long years before David's reign, notably in the days of the judges, the entering-in failure was conspicuous. Then there was a fresh appeal in Psalm 95 for a change for the better which we see in Israel's condition for a period of years thereafter. '"Today," God pleaded, '"if you will hear His voice, do not harden your hearts"'. So now we know from Hebrews 4 that Psalm 95 and probably others around it in the Psalter were composed by David, though not so attributed in our Bibles. David's bringing up of the Ark of God to what was to be truly its resting place for the nation settled in the land, namely to Zion, pictures God's purpose for a people at rest in His purposes.

Which brings us to the solemn matter of the source of the failure to 'enter in'. God's plea in David's day was, as shown above from Hebrews 4, that God's people should not harden their hearts after having heard God's voice and initially responded to it. Such a gracious and appealing God as ours speaks and speaks again in pleading for His people's ear and attention. He does so in all generations and covenant contexts. The 'today' of Psalm 95, as quoted in Hebrews 4, tells eloquently of God's constant and unfailing appeal of love.

What then were the underlying sins inclining the people to hardening of heart; to a subtle and progressive insensitivity to the word and will of God? They were simply the 'root' sins of unbelief and disobedience, 'root' sins which produce 'fruit' sins of heart hardening and departure from the living God. The sin was indeed a subtle and progressive evil, just as the 'entering in' associated with God's rest was, and is, a continuing and progressive grace of spiritual life. Such things, of course, concern the hearts of individual disciples of the Lord. But the emphasis in Hebrews is on a creeping collective spiritual malaise which can weaken the entire fabric of the life and service of those whose loyalty and devotion God delights in as a people for His own possession. God looks for His people to be continually entering into the glories of His house – 'coming to Him as to a living stone ... you ... are being built up a spiritual house' (1 Pet.2:4,5); and of His kingdom – 'through many tribulations enter the kingdom of God' (Acts 14:22).

Let us be aware that unbelief and disobedience are both sins of the human will, as well as resulting from neglect and carelessness. The Scripture depicts the matter in very solemn terms. 'Beware, brethren, lest there be in any of you an evil heart of unbelief in departing from the living God' (Hebrews 3:12). It is to be hoped we have already made it clear that this is all speaking of a sanctified, redeemed people in their spiritual lives and in no way implying any question of loss of eternal life, the free gift of a covenant-keeping God to every believer in the Lord Jesus Christ. But disciples in churches of God, comprising the people of God in the truly scriptural sense of 'the faith' which was 'once for all delivered to the saints' (Jude v.3) should be assured of their positional soundness concerning the house and kingdom of God. The glory of the Rest of God of which we are now speaking is summed up in the beautiful language of Psalm 27:4: 'One thing I have desired of the Lord, That will I seek: That I may dwell in the house of the LORD all the days of my life, to behold the beauty of the LORD, and to inquire in His temple.'

Dwelling; beholding; inquiring. Not doubting, disbelieving the clear word of Scripture and in consequence drifting into disobedience regarding the commandments of the Lord. Let us remember that the solemn and precious things we have considered concerning the Rest of God, flow in Hebrews 3, out of the stirring opening of that passage of the epistle where the Lord Jesus is presented as 'the Apostle and High Priest of our confession' and 'Christ as a son, over his house; whose house are we, if we hold fast our boldness and the glorying of our hope firm unto the end' (RV).

The high ways we have traversed,

And come to Zion's hill,

Where God, our God, is with us,

His purpose to fulfil.

(C.M. Luxmoore)

CHAPTER SIX: THE CHURCH (JOHN KERR)

———

In the introductory chapter of this book the writer briefly drew readers' attention to the 'varying uses of the word 'church' ...'. He emphasised the difference between the terms 'the church which is the body of Christ' and 'church of God', then added that many believers saw no difference. Presumably, he was referring to the fact that many thought these were interchangeable terms used to describe the same persons. One of the main thrusts of this chapter will be to show that differences do exist and to discuss which persons are in these churches. We will then develop the thought, also expressed in the first chapter, that these different terms 'contain separate treasures and we will look for the special values God intended us to see in each'. Finally, to help us practically in our Christian lives, we will consider the behaviour expected of those who bear these precious names which link believers to both the Saviour and God Himself. However, before doing so, we must establish the root meaning of the word 'church'.

Of all the scriptural terms being considered, probably the most common one is 'the church'. In fact, in its common English usage it is regularly used to identify the place of Christian worship, whereas in the Scriptures it is always used to describe the people who are gathered together: it is never used to describe a building or meeting place. Most Bible students know that the word 'church' is made up from two words in Greek which are 'ek' and 'klesis'. This quote explains the Greek in more detail; 'ekklesia NT:1577, from ek, 'out of' and klesis, 'a calling' (kaleo, 'to call'), was used among the Greeks of a body of citizens 'gathered' to discuss the affairs of state, Acts 19:39 ... It has two applications to companies of Christians, (a) to the whole company of the redeemed throughout the present era, the company of which Christ said, 'I will build My Church' Mat.16:18, and which is further described as 'The Church which is His Body', Ephesians 1:22,23;5:23, (b) in the singular number (e.g. Matthew 18:17, RV margin, 'congregation'), to a company consisting of professed believers, e.g. Acts 20:28; 1 Corinthians 1:2; Galatians 1:13; 1 Thessalonians 1:1; 2 Thessalonians 1:1; 1 Timothy 3:5, and in the plural, with reference to churches in a district.'(1) While this definition is helpful for defining the meaning of the word 'church' we need to study its use in more detail to understand who, exactly, are being described.

Now, at least as far as the Bible is concerned, we can state that any church is a group of people called out and subsequently gathered together. This is fundamental to our understanding of its varied use. As we study the use of the word we will think of three things in any particular usage, (a) who are the people described by the word, (b) what are they called out from, and (c) what are they gathered to? Let us now look at one use of the word 'church' that takes us back to the Old Testament.

Acts 7:38 is an interesting scripture for us to begin with. This 'church in the wilderness', KJV (or 'congregation' as some versions including the NKJV translate 'ekklesia' here) is a very clear reference to the Israelites who composed the camp of God in the wilderness under Moses' leadership. These persons were called out (v.36), received living oracles (v.38) and had a divine service in the tabernacle (v.44). Who were they? They were the re-deemed of the Lord (2). Where had they been called from? Out of Egypt (a type of 'the world'). For what purpose were they gathered together? To be God's own special people, a treasure He could call His own (3). This was accomplished through the Passover lamb (4), baptism (5) and their constitution as God's people on the basis of obedience (6), with a divine form of gov-ernment (7). As a result they were to be separated from all others (8).

The word 'church' in the majority of uses in the New Testament refers to what we have already mentioned: that which is called 'The Church the Body of Christ' and the 'Church of God'; the latter usually in a given location, e.g. Corinth. Other uses are 'the churches of God' (9), obviously referring to more than one Church of God and 'the church of the living God' (10) linked with the term 'God's House', describing the Churches of God in aggregate. Since the first two terms are the most numerous in the New Testament, and possibly the ones most misunderstood, we will restrict our comments to these.

Although there are many similarities between the Church the Body and a church of God (for example each reflect the same characteristics and the same persons can be in both at the one time), we will see that these are two separate entities. The fact that they are different will be shown shortly, but an illustration is a good starting point. To explain the difference, consider two separate entities, say we call them the London Police Force and the London Police Force Football Team. Each has a different constitution, different rules, and exists for a different purpose.

Nevertheless they have similarities and, like the churches under consideration, some people can be in both at the same time. I should imagine one similarity would be that the standard of behaviour in each is expected to reflect the integrity and honourable conduct imposed by the Chief Commissioner of Police.

We might say that the football team, although existing for a different purpose from that of the force is very closely associated with it. Any person can be in the force subject to qualifying for entry; however a person cannot be in the football team unless he or she is in the police force. All in the force are not in the football team; there are qualifications for that as well, namely a commitment to football which is not necessarily of interest to all police personnel.

If we now look at what the Scriptures have to say about the two churches referred to, it will become clear how the illustration helps. Like all illustrations it falls short in that not all in the force are expected to be in the football team, whereas most certainly all in the Church the Body are expected to be in a church of God during their lifetime.

Several characteristics of these two churches are shown by Scripture to mark them out as different entities, but, for brevity, we will confine ourselves to one topic, namely that a person can be in one and not in the other. Surely that would be enough to show they were different. Although most believers in the New Testament churches were in both, some were not (11) - just like the police force and its football team. Who then are in the Church, the Body of Christ?

The answer is those who are Christ's: believers in the Lord Jesus who have accepted Him as their personal Saviour; no other condition is required (12). They have been 'called out' and separated from the unregenerate and gathered together into a spiritual union with Christ (13). The objective: to be Christ's mystical bride which will one day be presented complete and perfect to Himself (14). Once in this eternal union with Christ it is impossible to lose that position (15), even if after salvation we progress no further in spiritual things and indeed fall back into disobedience and unbelief.

The description above of the Body of Christ is accepted almost universally among believers. However, when we come to consider what the Scriptures teach about a church of God, there are different opinions. So who were in a church of God? Saved people certainly, but saved people who had been baptised and added to churches of God (16). This was in obedience to Christ's teaching as communicated to the apostles by the Lord Jesus during the forty days He appeared to them, teaching 'the things pertaining to the kingdom of God' (Acts 1:3). This forms the pattern of the first church of God.

Those in that Church at Jerusalem were called out and separated, but from whom? Well, the fact that a saved man was put out of the Church of God in Corinth for sinful conduct (17), because he was disobedient to the apostles' teaching, shows that those in that church were called out and separated, among other things, from disobedient believers. This not only applied to moral disobedience, but also doctrinal (18). Those put away from a church of God were still in the Church the Body. So what were those in Churches of God gathered together to? They were gathered together to obedience and subjection to the Lordship of Christ (19).

Some believe that 1 Corinthians 1:2 shows that all believers everywhere who call upon Jesus' name, are in a church of God because they are in the Body of Christ and that a church of God is simply an aspect of it. We must, however, take into account the steps by which a person enters a church of God, namely through conversion, baptism and addition, then maintains that position. Believers outside the churches in New Testament times were surely not included in Paul's uncompromising description, 'all who in every place call on the name of Jesus Christ our Lord, both theirs and ours'. These latter were persons who owned the Lordship of Christ and were continuing in other churches of God in fellowship with each other (20) so that the letters to the churches could be passed around (21). Why should it be any different today?

In 1 Corinthians 12:27 (another verse often misunderstood) the Church of God in Corinth was not 'the' Body of Christ but 'body of Christ'. This puts an entirely different meaning on the verse. The Wycliffe Bible Commentary says 'The body of Christ (literally, body of Christ; there is no definite article) does not refer to the local church at Corinth, for there are not many bodies, a thought contrary to the context. Rather, it points to the quality of the whole, which each of them individually helps to constitute' (22). In the same chapter, verses 28-31 refer to gifts given to the Body, the divine plan being that these were manifested in churches of God, which were the visible representation of the Church the Body.

Let us finish by considering the wonderful privileges we have as a result of being called by these names. The Church the Body of Christ compares a spiritual reality with the working of the human body. Christ the Head, we the members, interdependent on each other under the 'headship' of Christ. Coming now to the Church of God, it is such an honour to be 'tagged' with God's name, to carry it in testimony and be known publicly with the appellation 'of God'. What responsibilities we have by being identified with God and Christ in these names!

(Bible quotations are from the NKJV)

1) Vine's Expository Dictionary of Biblical Words, Copyright (c)1985, Thomas Nelson Publishers. (2) Exodus 5:13 (3) Deuteronomy 7:6-7 (4) Exodus 12:21-23 (5) 1 Corinthians 10:2 (6) Exodus 24:7 (7) Exodus 24:12 (8) Exodus 33:16 (9) 1 Thessalonians 2:14 (10) 1 Timothy 3:15 (11) 1 Corinthians 5:13 (12) 1 Corinthians 12:13, Ephesians 2:16 (13) 1 Corinthians 12:13 (14) Ephesians 5:27 (15) John 10:28 (16) Acts 2:41-42 (17) 1 Corinthians 5:13 (18) 2 Timothy 2:18 (19) Colossians 2:6 (20) 1 Corinthians 1:9 (21) Acts 15:23 (22) The Wycliffe Bible Commentary. Copyright(c)1962 by Moody Press (23) Colossians 1:9-10

CHAPTER SEVEN: THE HOLY NATION (MARTIN DYER)

———

Levels of Association

In Genesis 2:18, God stated a principle that He intended should apply, not only to Adam, but also to Adam's posterity: "It is not good for the man to be alone; I will make him a helper suitable for him" (NASB). God had created Adam and recognised his spiritual, physical and emotional needs. He knew that Adam and his seed could find true fulfilment and satisfaction only in a life lived in fellowship and harmony with others. This of course applied to Adam's relationship with God, as well as to Eve. God ordained different levels of association to further His purpose that man should not be alone. The first fundamental one was that of marriage, from which would spring the family circle, 'God sets the solitary in families' (Psalm 68:6).

The grouping of families into tribes in Israel would seem to have divine sanction from Psalm 78:55, 'He also drove out the nations before them, ... and made the tribes of Israel dwell in their tents.' An association of families and common language gave rise to nations as we can see from Genesis 10:5. In a world of violence and unrest, an association of people was vital for security; a pooling of labour and ideas giving added strength and vitality to growth and development. Involved in all this were the establishment of government and the rule of law, with subjection to its laws and penalties when the law was broken. Genesis chapter ten is instructive in all of this; the early verses of the chapter showing that this development was according to divine purpose for the good and blessing of mankind.

The Origins of the Nation of Israel

In this early evolution of nations, God had in view another nation that would arise in due course. 'When the Most High divided their inheritance to the nations, when He separated the sons of Adam, he set the boundaries of the peoples according to the number of the children of Israel.' (Deuteronomy 32:8). We trace the origins of this nation back to the dealings of God with Abraham in Genesis chapter twelve. There was a command from the Lord to Abraham to leave his country and go to a land that God would show him. With the command was also a promise of blessing to him and to a nation that would spring from him - the nation of Israel. Linked to the promise was the intention that this nation would be a source of blessing to all the families of the earth. We can judge the importance of this purpose in the mind of the Lord, by the fact that it is mentioned four times.

Coupled to the command, Abraham's obedience, and the promise, was a covenant that God made with Abraham concerning his seed and the land that would be given to them (Genesis 15:18). This covenant was associated with sacrifice and the shedding of blood, telling us of its solemn nature for both parties, and bringing a guarantee of fulfilment. Consequent to these things, a foundation was laid that would govern the future relationship between God and the nation of Israel, including a nation mentioned in the New Testament scriptures. He would give them His Word, they should be obedient to it, and in that obedience they would be blessed and be a blessing to others.

A Nation Separated to the Word of God

In Exodus chapter 19 we find Israel, recently delivered from slavery in Egypt, now established as a nation, four hundred and thirty years from the call and promise to Abraham. In verses 5 and 6 the Lord speaks to them about His Word, their obedience to Him, and His promise of the honour and dignity He would confer upon them. In their obedience to the Lord they would be "a special treasure to Me above all people; for all the earth is Mine. And you shall be to Me a kingdom of priests and a holy nation." The Lord gives to Israel a distinctive label which marks them out from all other peoples and nations, 'You shall therefore be holy, for I am holy' (Leviticus 11:45).

The word 'holy' in these verses is in the original Hebrew the word 'qadosh' which means separate or set apart. The nation was to be different from all other nations, the law of the Lord regulating their worship, and their everyday life (Leviticus 11 and 19:19). In Exodus chapter 24, Israel pledged obedience and the Lord entered into a covenant with them based on His Word to them and their words to Him, a covenant solemnized by sacrifice and the shedding of blood. The blood being sprinkled on the people (verses 7 and 8) and on the book (Hebrews 9:19) gave a sacred link between the Word of the Lord and the acquiescence of the nation.

Only in this holy and separated condition was it possible for God to dwell among them, first in the tabernacle in the wilder-

ness, then in the Land at Shiloh and later in the Temple at
Jerusalem. His name was to be associated with His dwelling
place as we see from such scriptures as Deuteronomy 12:5 and 1
Kings 8:29. Psalm 111:9 tells us, 'holy and awesome is His name',
therefore the nation that worshipped at the Place of the Name
must be a holy nation separated to God. Balaam put it succinctly
in Numbers 23:9, 'A people dwelling alone, not reckoning itself
among the nations.'

Another Nation

Coming to New Testament times we find in Matthew 21:43 a
statement from the Lord addressed to the chief priests and elders
of Israel: "The kingdom of God will be taken from you and giv-
en to a nation bearing the fruits of it." We link with this a related statement to the Jews in Matthew 23:38, "See! Your house is
left to you desolate"; clearly a change was pending in the dealings
of the Lord with Israel. Because of a national turning aside from
His Word and a rejection of His Son, God was now looking to
another nation that would give to Him what He found wanting
in Israel.

The words of the Lord in John 4:21-24 indicate the nature of
the change. Jerusalem and the Temple would no longer be the
place of priestly service and worship, "the true worshipers will
worship the Father in spirit and truth". The days of a material
house and animal sacrifices were passing and "a dwelling place of
God in the Spirit" (Ephesians 2:22), and "spiritual sacrifices" (1
Peter 2:5) were being introduced. These changes would be integral to the nation that the Lord referred to in Matthew 21:43.
This nation too would be a 'holy nation' (1 Peter 2:9), reflecting

the unchanging character of a holy God. In chapter 1:2 of this epistle Peter refers to a 'sanctification of the Spirit, for obedience and sprinkling of the blood of Jesus Christ'. In Hebrews 12:24 the writer refers to 'Jesus the Mediator of the new covenant, and to the blood of sprinkling that speaks better things than that of Abel'.

The covenant with Israel was dedicated with blood (Hebrews 9:18). The Lord Jesus is the surety of the new and better covenant (Hebrews 7:22), as He said in the upper room, "the new covenant in My blood" (Luke 22:20). These scriptures remind us of Genesis chapters 12 and 15, and Exodus chapters 19 and 24. Thus we have replicated in the New Testament what was seen in the Old.

A New Testament Parallel

We find the origins and developments of this holy nation outlined in the book of Acts, and see a similar pattern of God revealing His will and an acceptance and obedience to His Word, as we saw in Abraham and in Israel. Between His resurrection and ascension to the Father, the Lord had spent forty days with His apostles 'speaking of the things pertaining to the kingdom of God' (Acts 1:3). He was giving guidance to these men with regard to the birth and growth of the nation He had referred to in Matthew 21:43. This holy nation had its inception on the day of Pentecost as recorded in Acts chapters 1 and 2, when the Holy Spirit came upon the 120 names who were together (Acts 1:15), and 'were all together in one place' (Acts 2:1 NASB).

Some 3000 souls received the word of the Lord that day through the preaching of Peter. They were baptized and added to the 120 and 'continued steadfastly in the apostles' teaching and fellowship, in the breaking of bread and the prayers' (Acts 2:41-42 RV). We are told in verse 44 that 'all that believed were together', and in verse 47 that 'the Lord was adding (Greek 'together') to their number day by day those who were being saved' (NASB). The word 'together' here is from the Greek phrase 'epi to auto' which tells us that all were 'of the same', i.e. they were united in a common purpose in the same place. These who were brought together formed the church of God in Jerusalem and were the nucleus of the evolving holy nation. As the disciples multiplied and were obedient to the faith (Acts 6:7), there was a development of churches of God being planted throughout Judea, Galilee and Samaria (Acts 9:31), in Antioch (Acts 11:19-26), and among the Gentiles (Acts 14:27).

The Expression of That Nation

All who were in the churches of God had responded to a call from God, through His Word, and were in a 'place'. They had been called "into the fellowship of his Son, Jesus Christ our Lord" (1 Corinthians 1:9). This was a community of churches, one in doctrine and practice forming the house of God, the place of the Name. Christ as God's Son and Great Priest has authority over it (Hebrews 3:6 and Hebrews 10:21). In this way God has found for Himself a holy nation, 'a people for his own possession, zealous for good deeds' (Titus 2:14 NASB), a people and a holy nation expressed in the churches of God today.

CHAPTER EIGHT: THE HOUSE OF GOD (JOHN ARCHIBALD)

———

We begin with the words of the great and wise King Solomon, 'But will God indeed dwell with mankind on the earth? Behold, heaven and the highest heaven cannot contain You; how much less this house which I have built' (2 Chronicles 6:18). It is indeed one of the most exciting truths revealed in the Scriptures: that God desires to have a dwelling place among His people on the earth.

The Tent in the Wilderness

We find this desire expressed to Moses at Sinai in the words, 'Let them construct a sanctuary for Me, that I may dwell among them. According to all that I am going to show you, as the pattern of the tabernacle and the pattern of all its furniture, just so you shall construct it' (Exodus 25:8,9). Here, like Solomon, we may well wonder at the grace and humility of God in this intention. He had mightily delivered the Israel people from the tyranny of Egypt, to make them His people, give them His laws, teach them how to serve Him and take them to the promised land. But it was also His purpose to dwell in the midst of their encampment in the wilderness. The Almighty who fills all heaven with His glory was to make His earthly dwelling place a tent that His people were to construct for Him!

At Mount Sinai the people of Israel became God's kingdom and nation when they pledged their obedience to His law and were sprinkled with the blood of the covenant that God made with them (Exodus 24:7,8). As part of this arrangement God gave them the pattern of how they were to serve Him collectively, centred on His sanctuary. Thus the people of Israel became uniquely God's possession among all the peoples of the earth.

In all of this it is important to recognize that they were not free to serve God in a manner of their own choice. God gave them detailed instructions about how they were to please Him. They were not given liberty to design the structure or choose the fabric and furnishings of His house. This is made clear in the words of God to Moses (see Hebrews 8:5).

The Temple in Jerusalem

Some five centuries later, David the king of Israel, a man after God's heart, had a deep and lifelong interest in God's dwelling place. When God had established him in his kingdom, he said to Nathan the prophet, 'See now, I dwell in a house of cedar, but the ark of God dwells within tent curtains' (2 Samuel 7:2). Although David was not permitted by God to build the temple, God's house had a very special place in his heart and writings. God showed him the place where it was to be built and gave him the plans for the building and its furnishing and the order of service within it. "All this," said David, "the LORD made me understand in writing by His hand upon me, all the details of this pattern" (1 Chronicles 28:19).

When King Solomon built the House of God in Mount Moriah at Jerusalem according to the pattern given to his father David, God placed His Name upon it, according to His word through

Moses, "But you shall seek the LORD at the place which the LORD your God will choose from all your tribes, to establish His name there for His dwelling, and there you shall come" (Deuteronomy 12:5).

The House of God in New Testament Times

The Old Covenant applied to an earthly nation, Israel, who served God in an earthly sanctuary. God's House then was a tent and later a building. As we read the New Testament, and particularly the letter to Hebrews, we learn that, under the New Covenant, God is served by a gathered people of heavenly citizenship who serve, not with earthly ritual in an earthly sanctuary, but have access to the sanctuary of God in heaven, under the High Priesthood of Christ. Under these circumstances, where and what is the practical expression of God's continuing desire to have a dwelling place on the earth? To answer this we turn first to:

1 Corinthians 3:16,17: "Do you not know that you are a temple of God and that the Spirit of God dwells in you? If any man destroys the temple of God, God will destroy him, for the temple of God is holy, and that is what you are."

The pronouns 'you' in these verses are plural in the original and so we understand that the persons in the Church of God in Corinth, to whom this letter is addressed (1:2), are the fabric of the temple or dwelling place of God. The absence of the definite article 'the' in the expression translated a temple of God indicates that the Church of God in Corinth was not the entire dwelling place of God on earth, but it would be wrong to assume that the Corinth church was one temple of God and that every other church of God was a separate temple of God. In the Scriptures the temple or house of God is never referred to in the plural.

So we understand that God has one dwelling place on the earth at any time. The literal translation of this expression would be 'you are temple of God'. We can also conclude from these verses that the temple or house of God is not the same thing as the church which is Christ's Body (Eph.1:22,23) of which every believer in Christ is a member, because that Church is indestructible (Mat.16:18).

1 Timothy 3:15: "I write so that you will know how one ought to conduct himself in the household of God, which is the church of the living God, the pillar and support of the truth." From this we learn that a high standard of behaviour is required of those who are in the house (or household) of God. In cases of serious sin, 1 Corinthians 5 deals with the necessity of putting such offenders out of the church and therefore out of the House of God. Here again the difference from the church the Body is evident since no-one can ever lose his/her place in that church.

The expression 'the living God' calls to mind the taunts of Elijah to the prophets of Baal on Mount Carmel, as they vainly and frantically besought Baal's response to their offerings. But a dead god is one that we could serve in any way we please without any scruples. The living God is not so, and it is His will that must prevail in His house and it is His commands that must be obeyed by those of His household. Here the title the church of the living

God is applied to the aggregate of all the churches of God on earth at the time.

1 Peter 2:3-5: "if you have tasted the kindness of the Lord. And coming to Him as to a living stone which has been rejected by men, but is choice and precious in the sight of God, you also, as living stones, are being built up as a spiritual house ... to offer up spiritual sacrifices acceptable to God through Jesus Christ."

1 Peter chapters 1 and 2 confirm and add precision to the ideas derived from the scriptures examined earlier. In chapter 1 Peter tells us a lot about the people to whom he is writing. They were believers in God (v.21), who had been redeemed with the precious blood of Christ (v.18,19), born again of the imperishable seed of the Word of God (v.23). This is why he calls them living stones in 2:5. But he also speaks of them obeying Jesus Christ and being sprinkled with His blood (1:2). The sprinkling of blood here has the same significance as it had for Israel in Exodus 24:8.

This sprinkling of the blood of Christ identifies the addressees of Peter's letter as the people of God under the New Covenant in recognition of their obedience to the teaching of Christ their Lord. It certainly means that they were baptised in water, for that is identified as the first pledge of obedience for disciples of Christ (Matthew 28:19,20), and that they were added to a church of God, for that is a step associated with and immediately following baptism in the teaching of the Lord (Acts 2:41). This addition, Peter describes in 2:4,5 as coming to the Lord as to a living stone and acknowledging His Lordship by being built up as a spiritual house for God. We note that the imagery of stones being built together to form a house certainly implies a close and ordered relationship between the stones deriving from the design of the building.

From these scriptures then, we conclude that God's dwelling place on earth in New Testament times, consists of believers in Christ who, acknowledging His Lordship, are placed in a conditional relationship with fellow disciples in churches of God. These churches in fellowship together form one community which God recognizes as His House. It is also clear that this conditional unity of disciples and churches is not the same thing as the Church the Body of Christ, which of course consists of all believers in Christ, whether or not they are in any visible fellowship with one another on earth.

The Importance of Exact Adherence to the Divine Pattern

We have seen the emphasis placed on following the divinely given pattern of God's House in the experience of Moses and David and have referenced the reiteration of the principle in the explanation of New Covenant service in the letter to the Hebrews (8:5). Men must always approach and serve God in His specified way and not according to their own ideas. Failure to recognize this has been a besetting problem in the entire history of mankind's attempts to please God, and is the reason for the multitude of practices and forms of worship in the many Christian denominations today, sadly evincing a widespread departure from the simple order set out in the teaching and practice of the Lord and His apostles.

In all this well-meaning diversity of collective (and often devoted) Christian service it is sobering to reflect on the Lord's word, 'Behold, to obey is better than sacrifice' (1 Samuel 15:22). The pattern of God's House under the New Covenant is the God-given constitution, teaching and practices of the people (living stones built together) who are its fabric. It must be implemented accurately and fully if God is to feel at home in such a dwelling place.

Love for God's House

David said, 'O LORD, I love the habitation of Your house' (Psalm 26:8). The revelation that God had a place on earth in which He would dwell with His people was more precious to David than anything else. How much greater is the interest and the pleasure in this subject of our blessed Master Himself, who is Son over God's House (Hebrews 3:6). Of Him it is written: 'Zeal for Your house will consume me' (John 2:17). When we understand that the whole Being of the Son of God is eaten up with desire for God's House, how could we be indifferent to it or regard it as a truth of lesser importance or beauty?

Of course, anything of special value to the Lord will be relentlessly attacked by Satan who tries to obscure its significance in the minds of God's children, but the matter of collective worship and service in the right way, is important, and God's House is a vital subject. The Lord does have a pattern for that House and its service, and happy are those who find it and follow it (Psalm 84:4).

CHAPTER NINE: THE HOLY AND ROYAL PRIESTHOOD (IAN PENN)

———

According to the Scriptures, God has recognised four priesthoods to date. These are those of: Melchizedek; the sons of the tribe of Levi, known as the Levitical priesthood (of whom Aaron was the first high priest); the Lord Jesus Christ (Hebrews 7:1,11,24); and the priesthood in which believers today may find themselves, to which the adjectives 'holy' and 'royal' are distinctively attached (1 Peter 2:5,9). Examination of each of these shows how a person was made a priest, and that the priest's work was to represent men to God and God to men.

Melchizedek

Nothing is said specifically of how the mysterious monarch, Melchizedek, the first priest of God in the Scriptures, came to be made a priest. He is unique; this information being deliberately withheld for the reason given in Hebrews 7:3. His work, however, was not unique because he gave to Abraham and blessed him, and then he blessed God and received a tithe (Genesis 14:18-20). Thus, there were manward and godward aspects in both his words and works.

The Levitical Priesthood

This, the second priesthood, was not established until the children of Israel were first redeemed from Egypt; constituted the people of God, God's holy nation at Mount Sinai (Exodus 19:1-8;24:1-8); and given instructions for the building of the house of God (Exodus 25:1-27:21; 28:1-30:38; Exodus 40:12-16). When all was done according to the Law, the divine truth that priests of God belong to the nation of God and serve in the house of God, was seen for the first time on the earth. Israel had become a kingdom of priests.

Aaron and his successors were men, appointed by God, from and for men. Their functions were to offer godward the gifts and sacrifices of the people of God, and manward, to ensure that all the people were fit to serve God (Hebrews 5:1-4). This dual role given at Sinai was confirmed by Moses prior to his death (Deuteronomy 33:10) and continued to the end of the Old Testament scriptures. At that time God castigated the priests for their failure, in offering sub-standard offerings in the house of God (Malachi 1:6-14). Hand in hand with this, too, He condemned the priests for failure in their teaching and their duties of care towards the people. Indeed in his manward role, the priest is actually called the messenger of the Lord of Hosts (Malachi 2:4-9).

Both roles of the Levitical priesthood continued during the days of the Lord in His flesh, since we see Him honouring their work in the case of the cleansed leper (Matthew 8:1-4; Mark 1:40-44; Luke 5:12-14) and showing, also, how the priest was not to neglect to minister to the fallen (Luke 10:31). Then the kingdom was taken from Israel at the death of the Lord Jesus; it and the priesthood being replaced by those of the Lord and His New Covenant people.

The Priesthood of the Lord Jesus Christ

The priesthood of the Lord Jesus Christ, prophetically announced as a priest for ever after the order of Melchizedek (Psalm 110:4; Hebrews 7:24), is the third to be recognised by God. It replaced that of Aaron and his sons (Hebrews 7:11-25) and its superiority is the cause of the New Covenant, of which He is the Mediator, replacing the Old Covenant (Hebrews 7:12; 8:1-7; 12:24). The writer to the Hebrews compares and contrasts His high priesthood with that of Aaron and his sons both as to appointment and function. As to appointment, we learn that whatever the priesthood, a high priest and therefore a priest of God must be of human birth (Hebrews 5:1).

As such, he has a birthright to represent God to men and men to God (Hebrews 5:1). He is not a priest by birth, however, but subsequently must be called of God (Hebrews 5:4). He does not appoint himself, but must be appropriately sanctified, anointed and consecrated to his office by another (Hebrews 5:5) as was the Lord in resurrection (Hebrews 8:4-6; 5:7-10; 6:19-20).

As far as representing men to God is concerned, unlike Aaron, the Lord offers only gifts because He dealt with sin once and for ever at Calvary (Hebrews 5:1-2; 10:1-14). In addition, the Lord has no sin and there is nothing to correspond in His priesthood with that of priestly sin under the order of Aaron (Hebrews 7:26-28). But He must have something to offer from the people of God today since He officiates on their behalf (Hebrews 8:1-3). As representing God to man, Aaron had to deal gently with the ignorant and erring, ministering to the people to fit them for service to God (Hebrews 5:2). The Lord ministers similarly on behalf of the people of God, but the basis of His care is very different. Circumspection figured prominently in the Aaronic priest's care because he was at heart no better than his fellows. The Lord, though knowing the weakness of our frame, and having been tempted in all points as we, triumphantly endured temptation and devilish onslaught (Hebrews 4:15). His is a victorious example completely to be followed (Hebrews 5:7-9).

The Priesthood of the People of God Today

Peter wrote to baptised believers (1 Peter 3:21) living in various, contiguous, Roman provinces (1 Peter 1:1-2) who had been brought together as one spiritual nation, people and priesthood (1 Peter 2:5, 9). Each and all were in one flock under the rule of overseers (1 Peter 5:1-11). John wrote to the seven churches in Asia, only one of those districts, identifying them as part of the same kingdom. As did Peter, John spoke first of their salvation by faith and subsequently that they were made a kingdom and priests in that same priesthood (Revelation 1:4-6). Paul spoke to men who were overseers in but one church in that district of Asia, the church of God in Ephesus. Whilst there, he had preached not only the gospel of salvation from hell (Acts 20:21), but also concerning the kingdom and the whole counsel of God.

The outcome of his work was to establish that local assembly as part of the flock of God tended by those overseers (Acts 20:25-28). Thus, whether viewed as a single assembly, a district of assemblies, or a collection of districts, the same structural unity is evident throughout the nation. Believers in all the churches of God composed the house of God, the kingdom of God, the flock of God, the people of God, God's holy nation.

So, the fourth priesthood (those for whom the Lord ministers as Great High Priest today) is composed of believers in churches of God comprising the house of God. Such have received His kingdom in succession to Israel, as promised in the parable of the vineyard, and as the Lord promised to His little flock (Matthew 21:33-46; Acts 4:5-12; Luke 12:31-32; Hebrews 3:1-6;7:26;8:1-3;10:19-25;12:18-29;13:10-16). It is the kingdom associated with the Mount Zion that is above, its heavenly Jerusalem and the 'true tabernacle'. As with the Levitical Priesthood, its 'service', is variously translated in the New Testament as 'worship', 'divine service', or 'ministering' (Hebrews 8:2;9:14;12:27-29; see Philippians 3:3).

Holy and Royal Priesthood Service Today

Within that house, in holy priesthood capacity, believers are able to offer up 'spiritual sacrifices acceptable to God, through Jesus Christ' (1 Peter2:5; the Great High Priest), that is, 'a sacrifice of praise to God ... the fruit of lips which make confession to his name' (Hebrews 13:15).

They do so at the Remembrance of the Lord Jesus Christ when they enter into the Holies where He has gone as their forerunner having made propitiation for their sins (Hebrews 2:17-18; 6:20; 9:25, 10:19-23). From these things we see also that, though of a different priesthood, the Great High Priest officiates in the heavenly sanctuary (Hebrews 8:1-5) on behalf of the priesthood of believers in the house of God today whose praise He leads (Hebrews 2:12). They worship by keeping today's ordinances of divine service just as much as Aaron and his sons kept those of their day (Hebrews 9:1)

But the priesthood is also a royal one and its function is to tell men of the excellencies of their High Priest, the King of Kings. The terms associated with this function confirm that this New Covenant people are the literal successors of those similarly described under the Old Covenant (cp.1 Peter 2:9 and Exodus 19:5-6) but also govern the approach to royal priesthood service. So the messenger of the Lord of hosts has to carry out his service in conformity with the laws that govern his nation. In particular, he must accept the discipline of working with his fellows and must do nothing to prejudice the standards and agreements accepted under God by them (as for example Acts 15:22-34;16:4).

He will receive help and succour from his High Priest in the difficulties of such service because, as far as possible, he must do no wrong nor work with wrong-doers (2 Corinthians 6:14-7:1; Hebrews 2:17-18;4:14-16;7:25). In sum, he should operate from within the churches of God and be subject to the rule of overseers (Hebrews 13:17). The apostle Paul certainly saw his service as a priest to be so even though his former associates thought he belonged to a mere sect (Acts 24:14). Paul declared his position boldly in the unlikeliest of circumstances far removed from entering into the Holies (Acts 27:23). He saw clearly that it was a service to do with the gospel of Christ (Romans 1:9) and expected all in the Church of God in Rome (and indeed in all churches of God) to be similarly committed (Romans 12:1-2).

Though these dual roles of all priesthoods are deliberately named and discrete in today's priesthood (1 Peter 2:5,9) they are closely connected, being sometimes, literally, set out side by side in the Scriptures. For example, in the diagnostic criteria of the first and of every church of God, service godward at the breaking of the bread, is linked with service manward, at the assembly prayer meeting (Acts 2:42). Similarly, the exhortation to enter into the holy place in worship to God is immediately followed by the instruction concerning love and good works to man (Hebrews 10:19-25).

Then again, following the instruction to service Godward in spiritual sacrifice, a complementary exhortation to 'do good and communicate' to man is given and is actually termed a sacrifice (Hebrews 13:15-16). Indeed the two aspects of service, on occasion, are more inextricably linked, because the offering up of sacrifice to God at the Remembrance simultaneously proclaims the Lord's death to the whole world (1 Corinthians 11:26) and what is said during that ordinance of divine service is to be for the listeners as well as primarily for the Lord (1 Corinthians 14:26).

(All Bible quotations are from the R.V.)

CHAPTER TEN: THE KINGDOM OF GOD (GEORGE PRASHER)

―――

The sons of Korah acclaimed God as "a great King over all the earth" (Psalm 47:2). As to His universal sovereignty and power, that remains abidingly true. Yet early in human history the majority of mankind chose to disown their allegiance to God, and as a result He "scattered them abroad over the face of all the earth" (Genesis 11:9), "having determined ... the boundaries of their dwellings" (Acts 17:26 NASB).

It was not until the time of Moses that there emerged the purpose of God to establish a nation which would uniquely be constituted as 'the kingdom of God'. God Himself would be their Ruler. His revealed law would be their constitution. Faithful obedience to that law would bring prosperity; disobedience would result in God's chastening.

Privilege Conditional on Obedience

Israel's formal acceptance of the responsibilities inherent in their becoming the kingdom of God is described in Exodus chapter 24:1-8. Having been redeemed from the tyranny of Egypt, and 'baptized into Moses in the cloud and in the sea' (1 Corinthians 10:2), they entered into a solemn covenant before Jehovah. When Moses had read to the people all the words of the LORD, and all the judgements, they declared, "All that the LORD has said we will do, and be obedient." And Moses took the blood, sprinkled it on the people, and said, "This is the blood of the covenant which the LORD has made with you according to all these words." This sequence of events is especially instructive. For redemption and baptism did not of themselves give Israel their status as the kingdom of God. There must also be understanding of His commandments regarding the order and service of His kingdom and a commitment to obedience to them.

Structured Administration

Under the leadership of Moses and Joshua the nation of Israel came into possession of the promised land by military conquest. Government was on a tribal basis, recognized judges and officers within each of the twelve tribes having responsibility for local affairs (Deuteronomy16:18). The Book of Deuteronomy records the care with which Moses was led by God to spell out for succeeding generations the legal framework that would maintain the administration of the kingdom of God as expressed through Israel. "You shall appoint judges and officers in all your gates, which the LORD your God gives you, according to your tribes, and they shall judge the people with just judgment" (Deuteronomy 16:18).

Spiritual Emphasis Within the Kingdom

A separate tribal region was not allocated to the Levites, but they were given forty-eight cities with adjacent pasture-lands. This arrangement was designed to provide a spiritual influence throughout the whole nation, for no one would live very far from one of the Levitical cities. From these cities the Levites would periodically travel to the place where the Tabernacle or

Temple of the LORD was located to undertake a course of service there.

Spiritual cohesion of the twelve tribes comprising God's kingdom was further promoted by the ordinance that three times in the year all males of responsible age were to appear before God: "Three times you shall keep a feast to Me in the year: ... the Feast of Unleavened Bread ... and the Feast of Harvest ... and the Feast of Ingathering", which fell at Passover, Pentecost and early autumn respectively (Exodus 23:14-17). When this requirement of the law was being observed every Israelite would be reminded that within God's kingdom priority must be given to spiritual consideration of His blessings, glorifying Him with praise and thanksgiving as the Source of all their material benefits.

Fluctuations in Obedience to the Covenant

Israel's record during the 1500 years from Moses to Christ was sadly flawed as to their divine appointment regarding the kingdom of God. First under a succession of judges, and then during the era of the kings of Israel and Judah, much depended on the lead given by those in power. The zenith of her influence was probably in the reign of King Solomon, of whom his father David said, "And of all my sons ... He has chosen my son Solomon to sit on the throne of the kingdom of the LORD over Israel" (1 Chronicles 28:5). We read also: "And all the kings of the earth sought the presence of Solomon to hear his wisdom, which God had put in his heart" (2 Chronicles 9:23). During those golden years, when Solomon was ruling in the fear of God, Israel's function as the kingdom of God found glorious expression, to the benefit of many other nations.

Yet in his later years Solomon sadly fell away in heart from Jehovah. This failure incurred God's judgment, so that ten of Israel's tribes rebelled against his son Rehoboam, who was left
with only the tribes of Judah and Benjamin within his kingdom.
The northern tribes lapsed into idolatry, forfeiting any possibil-
ity of continued association with the kingdom of God. Would
the Lord still recognize a small minority of the people of Israel
as fulfilling the role of the kingdom of God? Clearly, that was indeed the case! From this we learn the important principle that
even a minority who are enabled to fulfil God's revealed will as to
His rule among His people have a divine mandate in maintain-
ing the kingdom of God.

Suspension and Restoration

However, the disastrous time came when first the northern kingdom of Israel and later the kingdom of Judah were conquered
and most of the people carried away into captivity. The land was
left desolate, Jerusalem a heap of ruins. For seventy years the
kingdom of God was in abeyance. Such devotedly spiritual men
as Daniel preserved their personal dedication to Jehovah, but
lamented their lost privileges among a nation intended to fulfil
God's spiritual calling as His unique kingdom among all other
nations. The record of his prayer in Daniel chapter 9 reveals his
keen appreciation of God's justice in the chastisement which had
been visited on his nation, but also the prospect of restoration to
effectual service in the land as the kingdom of God.

That restoration was brought about by the return from Babylon
to the promised land of about 42,000 Jews under the leadership
of Zerubbabel and Jeshua (Ezra 2:64). They were strongly en-

couraged by God's word to them through the prophet Haggai: "Yet now be strong ... for I am with you ... According to the word that I covenanted with you when you came out of Egypt, so My Spirit remains among you" (Haggai 2:4,5). It was relatively "a day of small things" (Zechariah 4:10) but the principles of the kingdom of God could once more be viably expressed through the service of a remnant people.

The New Spiritual Kingdom

When some five centuries later the Lord Jesus was drawing towards the close of His ministry in Israel He warned that "the kingdom of God will be taken from you and given to a nation bearing the fruits of it" (Matthew 21:43). Through Israel's supreme sin in their rejection of the Son of God they forfeited their status as God's kingdom. To what other nation was the Lord referring to whom the kingdom would be given? He had said to His disciples, "Do not fear, little flock, for it is your Father's good pleasure to give you the kingdom" (Luke 12:32).

For a period of forty days during which He repeatedly appeared to the apostles after His resurrection He was 'speaking of the things pertaining to the kingdom of God' (Acts 1:3). He indicated that the apostles were to be His witnesses far beyond the boundaries of Israel – "to the end of the earth" (Acts 1:8). Their commission was to "make disciples of all the nations, baptizing them ... teaching them to observe all things that I have commanded you" (Matthew 28:19,20).

Faithful fulfilment of that commission by the apostles resulted in the rapid growth of a new spiritual people to which the kingdom of God was now given. They formed a trans-national unity of disciples of Christ, locally gathered in churches of God. This could not have been achieved by evangelism limited to leading souls to the Saviour, without emphasis on resulting obedience to His claims as Lord. Throughout the Book of the Acts, the apostles' ministry embraced "preaching the kingdom of God and teaching the things which concern the Lord Jesus Christ" (Acts 28:31).

As previously among the Israel nation, great importance was attached to a unifying structure of leadership. The quality of leadership was safeguarded by strict criteria for the recognition of elders or overseers and of deacons (e.g. 1 Timothy 3:1-13). Disciples in churches of God were enjoined to be subject to the leadership (Hebrews 13:17). The leaders themselves were to be subject to one another (1 Peter 5:5). When a critical difference arose about doctrine, representative elders from different areas met to seek God's guidance. Having been led by the Holy Spirit to a common understanding of the Lord's will, a statement was drawn up summarising the decision (Acts 15:1-29). As Paul and Silas re-visited the churches, 'they delivered to them the decrees to keep, which were determined by the apostles and elders at Jerusalem' (Acts 16:4).

Appropriate standards of behaviour were called for within God's kingdom. As Paul reminded the Corinthian church, 'Do you not know that the unrighteous will not inherit the kingdom of God? Do not be deceived. Neither fornicators ... nor thieves ... nor extortioners will inherit the kingdom of God' (1 Corinthians 6:9,10).

First Century Sunset

The apostles Paul and Peter both gave warning that after their departure spiritual declension would creep in among the churches of God (Acts 20:29,30; 2 Peter 2:1). Towards the close of the first century the apostle John wrote to seven surviving Churches of God in the Roman province of Asia a message from 'Him who loved us and washed us from our sins in His own blood, and has made us kings (NASB, a kingdom) and priests to His God and Father' (Revelation 1:5,6). John referred to himself as 'your brother and companion in the tribulation and kingdom and patience of Jesus Christ' (1:9).

This confirms that the kingdom of God was still continuing as expressed in surviving churches of God. For precisely how long is historically obscure. In divine mercy the recovery of truths outlined in this chapter make it possible for disciples of the Lord Jesus to be practically involved in the 'things concerning the kingdom of God' today!

CHAPTER ELEVEN: ASSEMBLY (GEOFF HYDON)

———

'Assembly' is an exciting word for Christians. It is the name for Christians when they are together. It is a hinge which allows the door of Christian activity to move. But a hinge has to be correctly positioned. We have first to get such fundamentals right, then we shall see how this precious, powerful truth very much needs to apply to us today.

The New Testament distinguishes between those who form a local church (ekklesia) of God and those who, while belonging to it, 'come together as a church' (Greek: en ekklesia). Ideally, these will be all those who form the church on a 24/7 basis, and, who, as such, are equally those who are scripturally required to continually devote themselves to assemble together for the various functions of a local church of God as commanded in the New Testament.

This should come as nothing new to readers of the Old Testament. But it will be very helpful to get back to the words the writers themselves used, since sometimes translations are not as precise as the original inspired text. A distinct word for 'assembly' is found frequently in the Old Testament, but not in the New. So when we move to the New Testament we must look for passages that use its essential meaning rather than the word itself. The thought 'assembly' expresses is certainly woven throughout the whole Bible.

Old Testament

In the Old Testament, the term 'assembly' most often applies to the people of Israel. It describes them when they gathered together. The first Bible reference to Israel as an assembly is Exodus 12:6, which speaks of the 'whole assembly of the congregation of Israel'; all Israel without exception (the congregation) were to assemble in their respective homes to keep the Passover. They were acting in unison in accordance to the command of the Lord, a key feature in the use of the term assembly. Now while they were in their tents in the wilderness, or in their houses in the Promised Land, they were all Israelites, 24/7. But at certain times the whole of Israel was called together (e.g. Deuteronomy 9:10), and as such they were then also described as an assembly.

An assembly did not necessarily include all Israel. You will see from reading 2 Chronicles 29 & 30 that at first the 'assembly' included only the king and princes, then the priest and Levites, then the people of Jerusalem and then all who responded to invitations to keep the Passover. The 'assembly' thus describes the group that responds to the command to meet at a specific time and place for a specific purpose.

The Hebrew word for such an assembly is 'qahal' (you can look it up in Strong's Concordance, number 6951). The purpose of these assemblies was always important. Israel had to assemble where and when they were told to do so, to worship God, to hear His directions for them, and to act in judgement against offenders. You will also notice as you study, that when the people speak with one voice to their leaders, they are called an assembly, for they must have gathered together to agree on what their representatives were to say (e.g. Numbers 16:2,3; 20:2-6).

We must stress that the assemblings of Israel were not accidental or even casual events. Also, they depended on the people's acknowledgment of the leaders used by the Lord to call the people together at God's command (Numbers 10:7). By contrast, at a low point in Israel's history the people were typified by independence; there was no acknowledged king and each of the people just did what was right in his own eyes (Judges 21:24,25).

You might in your study note a bit of a complication. The word 'qahal' is not always translated into English as 'assembly'. It is also translated as 'congregation'. However, there is a different Hebrew word that the Spirit of God has used when He wishes to refer simply to all Israel; it is the Hebrew word edah (Strong's number 5712), which is used 89 times in this way. It might have been helpful to us if this distinction in the original words 'qahal' and 'edah' had been consistently shown by using the different English words, assembly and congregation (in this respect the English Revised Version and the English Standard Version are indeed more consistent).

You will often find descriptions of the assembling of the congregation, but never 'the congregation of the assembly', because the congregation describes the whole, while the assembly describes those of a congregation that gather together (E.g. Exodus 12:6; 35:1; Numbers 1:18; 14:5; 16:19, 42; Joshua 18:1). In almost half of the references to congregation the term 'all the congregation' or 'the whole congregation' is used to further emphasize that congregation is meant to be very inclusive, whereas 'assembly' may exclude a portion of the congregation.

New Testament

Now this series is examining names applied to the same thing in both the Old Testament and the New. When the word 'church' in the New Testament is describing faithful Christian disciples in a particular city or town, the full term for that is 'the church of God in (City/Town)' (e.g. 1 Corinthians 1:2). If the New Testament had been written in Hebrew then these overall groupings might have been described by the word 'edah', because 'edah' refers to a whole congregation whether or not the people are all in the same place, at the same time, for the same reason. If you are in a church of God you are in it 24/7.

But Hebrews 10:25 reads: '... not forsaking our own assembling together, as is the habit of some, but encouraging one another; and all the more as you see the day drawing near'. Is this thought of assembling together a frequent and important theme in the New Testament - as it has been shown to be in the Old Testament? Yes, it certainly is. It is a vital hinge to the door of New Testament Christian activity.

God's Purpose

It is impossible to keep all the commands of our risen Lord Jesus Christ without gathering together. You will find important examples of a church of God gathering together in 1 Corinthians 11:17,18,20,33,34; 14:23,26, in these instances a single Greek word is used (Strong's number 4905). A concordance search of the word 'together' as used in the New Testament gets a bit complicated. But do not let that stop you doing thorough research. The complication is that whereas in English we express the thought in one word: 'together', in the language of the New Testament writer sometimes three Greek words were used to express the specific meaning of being 'together' as a church: 'epi to auto'. People who are 'epi to auto', together, are so by intent and purpose, not by accident but in order to be an assembly. You'll find examples of this in Acts 1:15; 2:44; 1 Corinthians 14:23.

Actions of an Assembly

We described this concept of an 'assembly' as a hinge in activities that God has designed to be engaged in collectively. That is why He provided the pattern for churches of God. So we will see in the above references for 'gathering together', key growth factors such as teaching, fellowship, worship, or prayer, or even judgement - which like pruning is necessary for effective quality growth. Leaders must gather the church for these purposes.

The commands of the Lord were passed on in the Apostles' teaching, and teaching is a vital requirement in our development as Christians. It opens our minds to greater obedience to Christ and greater service for Him (1 Timothy 4:6). The Spirit of God takes up the Word of God through the teacher (John 14:26; 16:13,14; 1 John 2:20). It is something that has its proper place in assembly gatherings, not only individual study (1 Corinthians 2:13; 4:17).

Paul, writing to the church of God in Corinth, speaks about them gathering together to keep the commands of the Lord Jesus Christ. So he says, 'when you come together as a church' (1

Corinthians 11:18). This is the church of God seen as 'en ekklesia' or in assembly. He then went on to teach them about their assembling to keep the remembrance, the high point of the worship of a church of God. It was a command of the Lord that necessitated disciples assembling together.

The importance of gathering together for assembly prayers is adequately shown from the example of the church of God in Philippi (Philippians 1:19). Their prayers were what Paul relied on for his effectiveness in gospel outreach. The door of opportunity relied in part on this hinge. Peter would have strongly endorsed the need for assembling for church prayer too! (Acts 12:5,12).

The church of God in Corinth also had to act collectively in judgment of an unrepentant immoral man. Paul emphasized to them that this action required them to be together (1 Corinthians 5:3-13). It was necessary for the 'leaven' to be removed from the assembly in this way, and its purifying effect was vital for the church to progress in holiness.

Not everyone in a church of God will necessarily be at all its meetings; a woman may be in labour, another may be away on a trip. The ones that gather, we may, with special aptness, designate as 'the assembly'. God's intention is that disciples of Christ should be together, together in intent, together in purpose and necessarily at certain agreed times together in the same place(s). This is part of His essential recipe for sustained effective growth. Trends toward independence will curtail that growth.

Let us not be satisfied with just the privilege of being part of the congregation. Let us dedicate ourselves in obedience to being part of the assembled company of the church, whenever it meets. This includes the assembly prayer meeting (Acts 2:42).

Did you love *A Bible Study of God's Names For His People*? Then you should read *Wisdom from a Watchman* by Jack Ferguson!

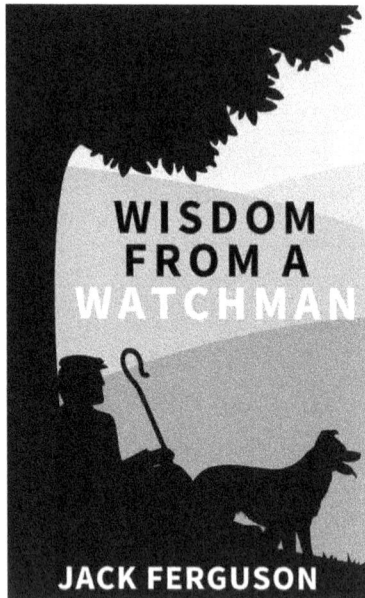

The late Jack Ferguson was known for being a "watchman on the walls", always alert to present or future dangers, challenges and opportunities for those that he pastored. This collection of some of his writings typifies his gentle, yet insightful ministry that is as perceptive now as it was when it was written.

Also by Hayes Press

Needed Truth
Needed Truth 1888
Needed Truth 2001
Needed Truth 2002
Needed Truth 2003
Needed Truth 2004
Needed Truth 2005
Needed Truth 2006
Needed Truth 2007
Needed Truth 2008
Needed Truth 2009
Needed Truth 2010
Needed Truth 2011
Needed Truth 2012
Needed Truth 2015
Needed Truth 1888-1988: A Centenary Review of Major
Themes

Standalone

The Road Through Calvary: 40 Devotional Readings
Lovers of God's House
Different Discipleship: Jesus' Sermon on the Mount
The House of God: Past, Present and Future
The Kingdom of God
Knowing God: His Names and Nature
Churches of God: Their Biblical Constitution and Functions
Four Books About Jesus
Collected Writings On ... Exploring Biblical Fellowship
Collected Writings On ... Exploring Biblical Hope
Collected Writings On ... The Cross of Christ
Builders for God
Collected Writings On ... Exploring Biblical Faithfulness
Collected Writings On ... Exploring Biblical Joy
Possessing the Land: Spiritual Lessons from Joshua
Collected Writings On ... Exploring Biblical Holiness
Collected Writings On ... Exploring Biblical Faith
Collected Writings On ... Exploring Biblical Love
These Three Remain...Exploring Biblical Faith, Hope and Love
The Teaching and Testimony of the Apostles
Pressure Points - Biblical Advice for 20 of Life's Biggest Challenges
More Than a Saviour: Exploring the Person and Work of Jesus
The Psalms: Volumes 1-4 Boxset
The Faith: Outlines of Scripture Doctrine
Key Doctrines of the Christian Gospel
Is There a Purpose to Life?
Bible Covenants 101
The Hidden Christ - Volume 2: Types and Shadows in Offerings and Sacrifices

The Hidden Christ Volume 1: Types and Shadows in the Old
Testament
The Hidden Christ - Volume 3: Types and Shadows in Genesis
Heavenly Meanings - The Parables of Jesus
Fisherman to Follower: The Life and Teaching of Simon Peter
Called to Serve: Lessons from the Levites
Needed Truth 2017 Issue 1
The Breaking of the Bread: Its History, Its Observance, Its
Meaning
Spiritual Revivals of the Bible
An Introduction to the Book of Hebrews
The Holy Spirit and the Believer
The Psalms: Volume 1 - Thoughts on Key Themes
The Psalms: Volume 2 - Exploring Key Elements
The Psalms: Volume 3 - Surveying Key Sections
The Psalms: Volume 4 - Savouring Choice Selections
Profiles of the Prophets
The Hidden Christ - Volumes 1-4 Box Set
The Hidden Christ - Volume 4: Types and Shadows in Israel's
Tabernacle
Baptism - Its Meaning and Teaching
Conflict and Controversy in the Church of God in Corinth
In the Shadow of Calvary: A Bible Study of John 12-17
Moses: God's Deliverer
Sparkling Facets: The Names and Titles of Jesus
A Little Book About Being Christlike
Keys to Church Growth
From Shepherd Boy to Sovereign: The Life of David
Back to Basics: A Guide to Essential Bible Teaching
An Introduction to the Holy Spirit
Israel and the Church in Bible Prophecy

"Growth and Fruit" and Other Writings by John Drain
15 Hot Topics For Today's Christian
Needed Truth Volume 2 1889
Studies on the Return of Christ
Studies on the Resurrection of Christ
Needed Truth Volume 3 1890
The Nations of the Old Testament: Their Relationship with Israel and Bible Prophecy
The Message of the Minor Prophets
Insights from Isaiah
The Bible - Its Inspiration and Authority
Lessons from Ezra and Nehemiah
A Bible Study of God's Names For His People

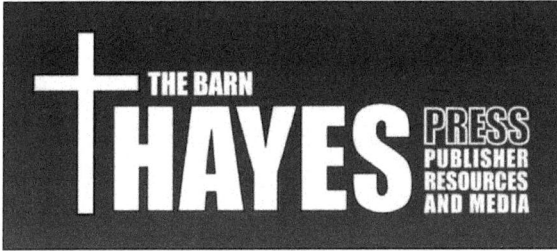

About the Publisher

Hayes Press (www.hayespress.org) is a registered charity in the United Kingdom, whose primary mission is to disseminate the Word of God, mainly through literature. It is one of the largest distributors of gospel tracts and leaflets in the United Kingdom, with over 100 titles and hundreds of thousands despatched annually. In addition to paperbacks and eBooks, Hayes Press also publishes Plus Eagles Wings, a fun and educational Bible magazine for children, and Golden Bells, a popular daily Bible reading calendar in wall or desk formats. Also available are over 100 Bibles in many different versions, shapes and sizes, Bible text posters and much more!

www.ingramcontent.com/pod-product-compliance
Lightning Source LLC
Chambersburg PA
CBHW060653030426
42337CB00017B/2590